Words From The Inner Chamber

Susie Farina

Words From The Inner Chamber
by Susie Farina

Printed in the United States of America

ISBN 978-1-60266-900-0

www.xulonpress.com

Dear Cindy,

for His
always listen for His
still small voice to you,
whisper I love to open
from the Inner Chambers of
His Heart!"

Blessings
Susie S. Harris
+
10/20/12

Words From The Inner Chamber
(Table Of Contents)

8) Dedication Page

9) Acknowledgement Page –

10) Gift Page

11) Words From The Inner Chamber
    (Introduction)

12) Words From My Most Secret Place
    (Introduction)

13) Words From My Heart To Yours
    (Introduction)

14) Words Of Warfare
    (Introduction)

15) Words Of Honor

This book is dedicated to my Father, Lord and Savior, Jesus Christ, who is my inspiration and without Him I would be nothing.

My Heart In His

His Love In Mine!

Thank You
I Love You Daddy

Susie Farina

Acknowledgements

This book is written for the divine purpose of giving God glory for all He has done. He has put such special people in my life. All glory honor and praise I give to Him.

Special thanks to –

My husband, Tony, who no matter what has always believed in me and never gave up. Your faithfulness and love to the Lord has been a light in the darkness for me.

My beautiful daughter, Amanda, for loving me through the hard times. Thank you for being my armor bearer in times of ministry. I love the woman of God you have become. You are my **_bestest_** friend!!!

My handsome son, Nathan, the most awesome man in my life. Thank you for having my back and taking such good care of me. God honors that!!!

To my biological father, Bill, who has gone on to be with the Lord but will always remain in my heart.

To my mom and dad, Eva and Norm who have prayed for me and encouraged me. I have drawn strength from the love you have poured into my life.

To my sister, Ellen, who has always been there for me time and time again. Our times of bonding will forever be a precious memory.

To my Pastor's, Justin and Yvonne, who have always had faith and trust in me. Thank you for encouraging me to go above and beyond my highest dreams and desires.

God's blessing upon you all.

I love you all so very much!!!

Susie Farina

This gift is given to:

_____

For:

_____

_____

Date:

_____

Words of encouragement:

_____

_____

_____

From:

_____

Words From The Inner Chamber is a collection of poems spoken to me by the Holy Spirit at various times in my life. They have been times when I've been up, down, happy or sad, discouraged or rejoicing. Some were spoken in the early morning hours while others were spoken during storms in the natural and spiritual. This one thing I know for sure that no matter what God has always been and always will be with me.

I am with you alway, even unto the ends of the world. AMEN.
(Matthew 28:20)

Words From The Inner Chamber

He speaks words from the inner chamber
They soothe my troubled soul
He speaks words of love and compassion
As they make my spirit whole
Sometimes I feel discontentment
As if my joy was all spent
But then He speaks to me
So soft and tenderly
My child it was for you
To the cross I went
I am with you always
To take your hurt and pain
I will replace it with a joy
Your spirit can't contain
So come into my inner chamber
And lay your cares at my feet
Enter into my rest
And your life will be complete

In His Chambers

What an awesome place to be
Here in the Master's chambers
To feel the heart beat of His love
Like the gentle flutter
Of the wings of a dove
I hear the precious whisper of His voice
That calms my spirit
And makes my soul rejoice
I see His eyes like flames of fire
They burn a passion in me
To live for Him my hearts desire
I sense His arms wrapped around me
Holding me in His embrace
It takes place in the Master's chambers
As I come and seek His face

A Voice From Above

Trapped inside
Nowhere to go
My mind all a mess
But why I didn't know
Ready to give it all up in death
I felt my soul yearning
And looking for rest
I want to be free
From this double mind
Traveling through life
Real peace to find
When to do myself in
I thought the right choice
It seemed I heard
A still small voice
It said to me
My child come here
I love you and want you
I've always been near
His voice was so gentle
So loving and kind
I knew right then
My peace I could find
Then I remembered
When I was a child
I was told I was His temple
And it would not be defiled
Right there once again
I gave my heart to the Lord
Now I'm standing on His promises
And trusting in His Word

Which Way

Lost and all alone my soul filled with strife
Searching for peace on the path of life
I come to a fork in the middle of the road
Which way do I turn to be free of this heavy load
I never had to make decisions by myself you see
I always had some one else to do it for me
Now I'm alone and scared I won't make the right choice
No one ever told me this would happen doesn't anyone have a
voice
Now there's no one around to help me decide
I wish there was a place I could just go and hide
The way to the left is full of laughter and fun
But it's not very bright and there isn't much sun
I haven't had much laughter on this journey of life
Just a lot of heartache and sorrow and strife
No valleys to walk through no hills to climb
Just living it up and having fun all the time
Now the path to the right it's quite a different place
It seems to be filled with God's mercy and grace
With all the hills and valleys it's not the easiest way to go
But challenge and adventure is a way I've come to know
So I'll take the path to the right I know it's the right choice
I just heard Him calling me because I've come to know His voice

Renewed Faith

Lord I couldn't begin to thank You
For All You've done for me
The promises You gave me
And setting my soul free
You've renewed my faith
And my strength in You
You have made all
My hearts desires come true
I couldn't do enough for You
To ever repay
The peace You give me
Day to day
You did all this
Because You love me so
Now I pray with You
I'll always go

The Giver Of Life

Take a look around you
And surely you will see
The giver of life is still giving
For He gave life to me
He takes me to the mountaintop
And fills my hungry soul
He takes me to the valley low
And makes my body whole
The Spirit that's inside of me
Gives me life anew each day
While He gently leads and guides me
As I follow in His way
You can have this life
That only God can give
Just tell Him that you love Him
And for Him you want to live
When you get His Spirit
Deep inside of you
You'll soon find out
That what I say is true
You can say to others
And your reply will be
The giver of life is still giving
For He gave life to me

Thank You

Thank You Lord for Your mercy
Thank You Lord for Your grace
My only hearts desire
Is to boldly seek Your face

You're worthy of my worship
You're worthy of my praise
You have changed my life completely
And I'll praise You all my days

As I come into Your presence
With a sacrifice of praise
My life is on the altar
As Your glory fills this place

I'll sing to You my Savior
I'll dance before Your throne
I'll glorify Your name o' Lord
And worship You alone

Through triumph and tragedy
Even in my own strategy
You've not left me alone
Now I bow before Your throne

Dance With My Father

I want to dance with my Father and feel His heart beat
I want to dance with my Father His love so sweet
I want to dance with my Father and as we stand face to face
I will feel His compassion and see His eyes filled with grace

As I dance with my Father I can feel His heart beat
As I dance with my Father I feel His love so sweet
As I dance with my Father and we stand face to face
I can feel His compassion and His eyes filled with grace

I love to dance with my Father because I feel His heart beat
I love to dance with my Father because His love is so sweet
I love to dance with my Father because as we stand face to face
I am filled with His compassion and I see His eyes filled with grace

The Holy of Holies

I enter into the Holy of Holies
It's a place where I am blessed
I find peace and contentment
Sweet solitude and rest
There's a passion and desire
That burns within my soul
I'll be alone with my Father
As His love will make me whole
There's a change that takes place
In my heart while I'm there
The deep secrets buried within me
With my Lord I can share
My hurts are all mended
My sins are erased
As I come into His throne room
And we stand face to face

In The Early Morning Hours

In the early morning hours
You call me to Your throne
I awaken from my slumber
Come into Your presence
To be alone
You speak so soft and tenderly
As You hear my hearts cry
You blow a kiss from heaven
For my eyes to dry
I feel Your arms around me
As I cling to Your embrace
Like a child with its Father
I turn to see Your face
It shines with love and compassion
As I feel an inner peace
I'm baptized in Your glory
As I feel a sweet release
For it's in the early morning hours
You speak to me Your will
As I come into Your presence
To my soul You whisper
Peace be still

In The Quiet Place

Lord You have called me
To a higher place in You
It's a quiet place where Your mercies
Everyday You renew
In the quiet place
I have no worries or strife
I can feel Your fresh anointing
So strong on my life
My strength is restored
As You pour oil from Your throne
In the quiet place my heart is surrendered
As I worship You alone

God's Beauty Within

You radiate such beauty
But it's buried deep within
No one else can see it
Quite the way I can
Your countenance it glows
And brightens up my day
It shines on darkened paths
To lighten some ones way
This beauty that's within you
I want all to see
Look deep inside your heart
For it is part of Me
I've made you for My pleasure
And oh what joy you bring
I take pride in My creation
To Me you're everything
I have placed a love within you
The world can't take away
As you open up your heart
It will grow from day to day
So let this beauty shine
For all the world to see
For when they look at you
They will see a part of Me

A Precious Treasure

You've given me the power
So I can do all things
Granted me Your strength
To soar with eagles wings
You've poured into me mercy
Bestowed upon me grace
You've given me the privilege
To boldly seek Your face
So now all that is within me
I come to honor You
I praise You and adore You
For Your love is true
I exalt You and adore You
I lift Your name on high
I glory in Your presence
As You hear my hearts cry
No diamond gold or earthly gem
Could ever quite compare
To the treasure You placed inside me
Your tender love and care

Blown By Your Spirit

I want to be blown by Your Spirit
Blown by Your Spirit
I want to be blown by Your Spirit
Cause me to ride upon
The winds of Your Spirit

As I am blown by Your Spirit
Blown by Your Spirit
As I am blown by Your Spirit
I will rise up high
On the winds of Your Spirit

With All My Heart

When I am in Your presence
And come to worship You
I get so overwhelmed
By the good things that You do
My mind starts to reflect
On all the great things You have done
The way You healed and saved me
And all the battles that have been won
You protected my heart from hurts
And very painful things
You caused me to be victorious
And soar with eagle's wings
I bow before You now
To give You honor that is due
I'm here with all my heart
To truly worship You

In His Image

As I gaze into the horizon
And see the setting of the sun
My heart is captured by Your presence
How awesome to be made
In the image of the Holy One
You spoke into existence
All of nature and its plan
Then with Your very breath
You breathed a living soul in man
My heart gets overwhelmed
By the miracle of it all
My spirit is filled with joy
As before You I stand in awe
Such a love so great a love
I wonder how can it be
That the very one who made heaven and earth
Has chose to dwell in me

Healing Touch

Thank You Lord for Your healing touch
I'm so grateful
Love You so much
I wouldn't want to live another day
If I wasn't able to praise Your name

You've touched my heart and touched my mind
A greater love I could never find
Love You so much
Love You so much
For Your healing touch

I Give Them Up

I give them up
I give them up
I give them up to You
My hurts my fears
My doubts my tears
I give them up to You

I give them up
I give them up
I give them up to You
All those things
I've held onto for years
I give them up to You

Fully Surrendered

I want to be fully surrendered
Fully surrendered to You
So that all that's left within me
Is my praise unto You

Take control of my heart and my soul
Fully surrendered to You
So that all that's left within me
Is my praise unto You

Matters Of The Heart

Here it is Lord
I give You my heart
I give it all
Not just a part
I place it in Your tender hands
As a sacrifice to You
To purify and cleanse it
And make it anew
You know it's been misused
And tattered and torn
There are places inside
That are crushed bruised and worn
Oh how my heart longs for Your gentle touch
With Your hands wrapped around it
I need You so much
Bind up those things
That have kept me from You
Clean out those things
That are impure and untrue
Cause Your kindness and love
And forgiveness to flow
Place within it Your desires
For me to will and to know
Let it be filled with compassion
Only you can impart
For the characters of You
Are the true matters of the heart

Tell Me

Tell me can you hear Him
His still and quiet voice
The one that speaks to your spirit
And makes your soul rejoice

Tell me can you see Him
The presence of our God
He's in the skies and seas
And in the very path you trod

Tell me can you smell Him
The sweet savor of our King
He's the smell of a gentle rain
That passes by in spring

Tell me can you touch Him
Can you feel the very beat of His heart
Do you sense His love and compassion
So from His presence you don't depart

Do you know He's always near you
In every thing you hear feel or see
Most of all can you see Him
As He lives inside of me

Only You

Turn my heart inside out
So the world can see
Your mercy love and grace
That's deep inside of me
Cause it to be my passion
To a world that's lost in sin
To let Your oil and wine
Pour out from me
To restore them to You once again
Let Your anointing power
Penetrate the heart of every being
Let Your glory manifest in me
So it's only You they are seeing

Empty

Empty me out till I'm full
Full of Your mercy and grace
Empty me out till I'm full
As I come and seek Your face

Empty me out like a well run dry
As before You I bow
Please hear my humble cry

Empty me out till I'm full
Full of Your mercy and grace
Empty me out till I'm full
As I boldly seek Your face

We Give Thanks

We're gathered round the table
With friends and family
To thank God for the blessings
He's given You and me
We thank Him for the food
He's placed before us this day
And for those that are dear to us
We met along life's way
We thank Him for blessing us
With health and prosperity
We even thank Him for giving us
A mind of clarity
We take this time to thank Him
For the grace and mercy He has shown
Some might even thank Him for the future
And for it's unknown
And as we stop to think of His goodness
We might even shed a tear
But tell me do you thank Him everyday
Or just this time of year

Through The Storm

Sometimes I feel like I'm being tossed
On the waves of an open sea
As deep within my soul
A storm rages inside of me
The cares of this world
Are like dark clouds that gather round
Sometimes the fear inside of me
Is like a mighty thunderous sound
It tries to drown out the gentle whisper
From the King of Glory's throne
Peace be still my child
You are not alone
Don't let the clouds fool you
Into thinking I'm not there
Don't allow the wind and rain
Flood your thought making you think I don't care
Just keep your eyes on me
Even though the dark clouds form
You know I'm with you always
Even through the storm

The Mighty Waterfall

Lord You pour Your Spirit into me
Like a mighty waterfall
Pushing through the hardest places
That I can't contain it all
It rushes through my worries
And even breaks my pride
Tearing down walls of fear and doubt
That I have built inside
Yet it calms my troubled spirit
And cleanses every part
Washing away unforgiveness
And bitterness in my heart
As I'm filled with Your Spirit
Your anointing is manifest
Touching the hearts of others
For their souls to be blessed
As Your anointing flows from me
To gain another's souls salvation
I pray that it continues through them
To reach for You a nation
So flood me with Your Spirit
Until Your love and power is shown
Use me for Your Kingdom Lord
To make Your glories known

Never Let Go

Don't turn back to the ways of the world
Keep hold of your faith and follow after God
He's walking right there by your side
To lead and guide you on the path you trod
Don't take your eyes off Him or lose your sight
For it's in His eyes you see His glory and might
Don't deafen your ear to His still small voice
As He speaks to you your soul will rejoice
Never let go of His mighty strong hand
Your Father wants to lead you to the Promised Land
Know that He is there in every situation
Just seek His kingdom and it's manifestation
It will relieve all of your sorrow and strife
And bring about righteousness joy and peace in your life

Have Faith

Faith is believing
Knowing
Having assurance
And confidence
That the Hope of Glory
Jesus Christ
And love of God
Abounds in your heart
As you fulfill
The divine purpose
Plan and destiny
That is set before you
By a loving
And compassionate Father

Into Captivity

Lord You've captured my heart
And the very being of my soul
There have been times
When You have taken full control
Those times to me have become so precious
All I want to do
Is lift my hands in worship
To truly honor You
No one else could ever experience
This love that I have known
Because it's a time of intimacy
Between You and me alone
It's not just in my mind
But it's captured deep within my heart
It's here within Your presence
New mercies You impart
So take me into captivity
And never let me go
As I surrender to Your will
It's Your heart I want to know

Never Alone

I know You are always with me
Every hour of every day
Walking right beside me
Even when I'm not following Your way
In the early morning hours
As I open up my eyes
And in the still and quiet of the night
You hear my lonely hearts cry
When feelings of solitude overwhelm me
And I think that I just can't cope
You come and wrap You arms around me
Your gentle touch gives me hope
While lying on my bed alone
Longing for someone to caress
I feel Your heart beat next to mine
It relieves all my fears and stress
There are times my soul is yearning
For the sweetness of a kiss
You gently take my hand and say
Come away with me I'll carry you through this
You have become my husband
My lover and a friend
I know You'll be here beside me
Until the very end

But For The Scars

See these scars they are there for a reason
Each one has a specific time and season
From battle to battle I've endured the pain
So why do I continue to fight
What is there to gain
Some are from hurts when loved ones I've lost
Some are from my own doing by giving up
And not counting the cost
There are scars from attacks of the enemy
And laying down my sword
Some are from not obeying and trusting in the Lord
But there is a beauty in these scars
That I have come to see
It's the beauty of the Lord as He's gently healing me
The closer I draw to Him
The deeper the healing He'll impart
It's then I hear the voice of God speaking to my heart
See these scars they are there for a reason
Each one has a specific time and season
I've endured your pain and bore it on the cross
It was My love for you so your soul would not be lost
So take your eyes off the scars and come and seek My face
Draw near to Me and enter into our secret place
But for the scars you would never know
That I could heal your pain
But for the cross you would never know
You have eternal life to gain

The Seasons Sing Your Praises

The fragrance of Your presence
Is like a sweet spring rain
It floods my heart and soul
With a joy I can't contain
I see Your awesome power
In a world created for me
It's in every blade of grass
To the mighty tall oak tree
Even the seasons sing Your praises
As they change at Your command
Nature displays Your beauty
In obedience to Your plan
Not a winter's snowflake as it falls
To the ground is ever quite the same
As each one softly glistens
And whispers the praises of Your name
In the spring time buds will blossom
To flowers in full bloom
Your mysteries unfold
In a summer storms dark clouds and gloom
The autumn is full of Your radiance
As it reflects and manifests Your love
With vibrant colors throughout the world
In water earth and sky above
All of nature shows Your wonder
And tells of creations story
As I look around I can see
That the whole earth is filled with Your glory

The Breath Of God

You breathe into me Your very breath
Deep within my soul
It gives me life from day to day
And makes my spirit whole
That very breath You give me
I return to You in praise
As it's stirred up within my spirit
Like mighty ocean waves
I can feel Your very heart beat
As it beats within my soul
It brings new life from day to day
I give You complete control
That very heartbeat You give me
I'll return worship unto You
For breath of life and a heart that beats
And the miracles You do
I'll love You with every breath I take
And I'll let my heart proclaim
You alone are worthy of my worship
As I praise Your Holy name

Breath Of Life

Let Your breath of life blow on me
Come and restore my soul
And set my spirit free
I return it back to You
In my worship and my praise
As it floods my soul
Like might ocean waves
I'll love You with every breath
And I will proclaim
You alone are worthy of my worship
As I praise Your Holy Name

Jesus my breath of life
You alone are worthy of my worship and my praise

Abba, Father, Jesus, Breath of Life
You alone are worthy of my worship and my praise

The Mercy Seat

I'm sitting here on the mercy seat
A place I'm not worthy of
Had it not been for Your precious grace
And unfailing love
I'm covered by Your angels
Underneath their wings
As they cry out, "Holy Holy Holy
I can hear them sweetly sing
While I sit here on the mercy seat
In the throne room of Your heart
You come and commune with me
And new mercies You impart
Here within Your presence
With the angels I sing praises to Your name
Holy Holy Holy is the Lord my God
Worthy worthy worthy
Is the Lamb forevermore proclaim

The Dry and Barren Place

I'm here once again in that desert place
Where everything seems so dry
I just don't understand its reason
So I question Lord **Why**
Feeling lost and confused
All alone without a friend
Trying not to despise this place
As I wonder is there no end
Parched in my spirit
I thirst for more of You
Wanting more of Your love
I weaken and struggle to get through
Then in the stillness of the night
When it seems I fight for my last breath
My faith is all gone
I can feel the hand of death
With Your Spirit like a sweet wine upon my lips
My thirst is quenched
As You show me this is a place You've called me
And in Your Spirit I'm drenched
Now I understand the reason
For this dry and barren place
You've drawn me by Your Spirit
To come and seek Your face
It's a place of sweet communion
As Your passion floods my soul
Because of Your grace and mercy
I'm able to give You full control
This place to which You have called me
Takes away all fear and strife
No longer seen as a place of death
But a place where I can now speak life

Wanting Nothing

Here I am wanting nothing
Just to be with You
Sitting in Your Holy presence
Is all I want to do
I'm just here to love You Lord
Not wanting anything
Sitting in Your Holy presence
The Holy presence of my King
A pure heart of praise and worship
Will be my embrace
As I come before You now
To humbly seek Your face
Receive my gift of worship
That I lay before Your throne
May it be a pleasing fragrance
As I am here with You alone

Just One Drop

While on the mountain God showed me
A drop of blood my salvation to impart
Yet He was wounded for my transgression
And bruised to cleanse my sinful heart
Beaten beyond recognition and a sword-pierced side
Until His heart was broken
Yet to prove His love for me
Not a word was spoken
If all it took was just one drop
Then tell me Lord which drop was I
Was it from the crown of thorns
Or from the tears of blood You cried
Then He spoke of just one drop
To cover my multitude of sin
All it took was that very first drop
For me to have His peace within
Just one drop that very first drop
Yet He bore it all for me
The cross the crown the forty stripes
To give me eternity

What If...

What if...
Jesus only loved us according to
Our desire to worship Him
Would our worship be deep and strong enough
For Him to want to die for our sin

What if...
He only blessed us
Due to our praises from our heart
Would our praise cause Him to give His life
And His love to us impart

What if...
God's grace only carried us according
To the measure of faith
How far would His grace carry us
A day, a week, a month

What if...
God's mercy was only given to us
For the mercy that we give
Would that mercy get us eternity
Forever with Him to live

What if...
He never blessed us and we had to rely
On our own strength to get us through
Would just knowing that He died for us
Be enough for us to give Him honor He is due

It's a good thing there are no "What ifs"
And God's grace and mercy are without measure
That should make us want to praise Him more
We need to see His love for us is a precious treasure

Like Fine Silver

Break me down until I'm nothing Lord
To restore me back to You
Polish me like fine silver
To let Your love shine through me
Empty me out of my selfish pride
And let Your grace and mercy be poured out
Fill me up with Your truth and faith
Ridding me of all fear and doubt
Teach me to trust You
No matter what circumstances come my way
I want to live in Your Kingdom
Of righteousness peace and joy each and every day

The Anointing

I don't have to seek Your anointing
For You are always pouring it out
If I don't feel Your presence
It's because of my own doubt
Your anointing is always flowing
Like a river running wild
So let Your anointing flow out of me
Hear this petition from the heart of Your child
I don't have to reach for something
That I cannot see
Because Jesus Christ the anointed One
Lives inside of me

His Peace

If you only knew what I go through
Each and every day
Trying to live my life to gain peace
In the midst of disarray
The battle isn't easy
Fighting against the sin
Sometimes I feel I don't have the strength
But there is a burning desire in me
Not to give up until I win
Some times it's often frightening
And fear plagues my mind
But then there's this peace
That passes all understanding
When I seek it I always find
For I know a man named Jesus
Who once laid down His life
As I trust Him I know
He will bring me through this strife
He brought me out before
And I know He'll do it again
He'll carry me through to triumph
The victory to win

The Spirit of Christmas

Sitting beside the Christmas tree
With all its bright lights and splendor
Causes me to think about
A little wooden manger
I think about the wise men
And how they followed that North Star
Then about the shepherds
Weary as they traveled from afar
Then I envision the smile on Mary's face
As she holds that little one
What a privilege and honor
To give birth to God's only Son
Then I think of the Spirit of Christmas
And how it's not just for one day
But it's the life death and resurrection
For a seeking soul today
He went from a wooden manger
To an old wooden cross
He did it all for us
So our souls would not be lost
The Spirit of Christmas is eternal
But we celebrate it just once a year
As we decorate our houses
And fill them with good cheer
Let us never forget the reason
He came into this world
He paid a price this blessed child
Our Savior and our Lord

Drinking From The Well

There's something in me
About ready to burst
Seeking Your face
Just instills in me a deeper thirst
I want to drink from Your wells
That will never run dry
A well that gives me strength
To live and not to die
The well of forgiveness
So I'm not full of selfish pride
Your well of transparency
So there's nothing to hide
If I don't drink from the wells
I'll have nothing to pour out
So flow through me
To free someone of fear and doubt
Let me drink from the wells
That flow wild and free
Pour Your mighty waves
Of mercy and grace out of me

Through The Gate

I enter into Your courts through the gate which is Christ my Lord
I cannot enter by any other means or any other way
I offer up to You a sacrifice as I place myself on the altar
For Your grace mercy and forgiveness I pray
There's a fresh anointing on my life
As I'm washed by the blood of the Lamb
An empty vessel I drink from a fountain that will never run dry
I eat from the table of communion and fellowship with the Great I
Am
I'm guided by a beautiful and glorious light that leads me to a
place of sweet intimacy with You
You touch the coals to my lips
Purifying my heart and my mind You renew
You call me beyond the veil and I seek Your face
I'm seated with You in the Most Holy Place
I hear angels cry Holy Holy Holy as they surround the seat of
mercy
Where You've invited me to sit
Your love and compassion shine like the sun
And my heart and life to You I commit
Things are all turned around
I see things in a new and different light
I now see from where I came to where I am today
What I've over come and how I've won each fight
As I look out and see that I've endured each test
I walk in Your fullness and a place of wholeness and rest

Just One Voice

I know what the enemy's trying to do
But it's not going to work this time
Pounding my thoughts with false illusions
Hopeless passions try to fill my mind
But I've finally learned the difference
I've come to know God's voice
I never really knew it before
And always seemed to make the wrong choice
Now I listen ever so closely
Because His voice is gentle and still
Like a whisper in the wind
He speaks to me His will
I'm not just going to listen this time
But I will obey
If I hearken to the other voice
It makes me want to stray
God has all the answers to my questions
And understands my doubts and fears
Yet He's still the one that comes
And wipes away my tears
So the false illusions I can do without
I don't need hopeless passions
My mind is stayed on the one
Who looks at me with a heart of love and compassion

Where God Is

I don't want to go back
To where I've already been
Because I've come too far
To begin again
I want to go
Where God wants to go
The glory of His presence
Is all I want to know
Time spent on the threshing floor
Prostrate before the Almighty One
The dark sin of my heart is trampled out
Like chaff blown in the wind it is gone
I want to build an altar
From the testimony of my tears
Where the foundation is Christ
Not my struggles or my fears
As I lay my life on the altar
To be cleansed and purified
I'll offer up a sweet sacrifice of praise
For God to be glorified

At Rest

To see a shimmer of Your glory
Or just one glimpse of Your face
Would satisfy this longing
As I worship in Your Holy place
Sitting in the heavenlies
Upon the seat where Your mercies flow
While resting in Your bosom
The love of my Father I've come to know
Your arms so gently wrapped around me
Caressing my soul frees me from all my fears
I sense the tender touch of Your hand
As it wipes away my tears
I can feel Your precious heart beat
As I lay my head upon Your chest
It beats with love and compassion
And causes my spirit to be at rest
My desire is to dwell in Your presence
No other place will do
There's no other place I'd rather be
Than just to be with You

Dry Bones

Walking in the valley of desolation
I can hardly catch my breath
My spirit is saddened
Because all I see is death
As I look around
All I see are so many dry bones
Then God shows me
These bones are my own
Some are dry and brittle
While others have turned to dust
But I've come so weak in my spirit
I've learned to adjust
Gathering all the strength I have within me
I give the Lord a shout
Lord I don't want to die in this barren place
There must be a way out
Then He says speak life to the dry bones
Even those that have turned to dust
If you don't want to die in the barren place
Speaking life is not an option but a must
So I started to speak life
Into the dry places
And I even spoke
Into the empty and dry spaces
The bones began to gain strength
And come together as one being
They started to walk in faith
And newness of life I was now seeing
As I gain strength and spoke life
Into each and every circumstance
I began to realize God didn't bring me
To this valley just by chance

The Makers Pruning

I'm just a little flower of innocent fragrance
Growing in a field
Wondering how will I grow
And what kind of seed will I yield
I want to be pleasing to my Maker
And grow in perfect form
But how can I with this wind and rain
Blowing against me from the storm
Sometimes the wind tears off one of my petals
That has gotten weak
Then the heavy rains they come
And cause one of my leaves to break
But one thing I can be sure of
Is that it has caused my roots to grow deep and strong
Lord when will this storm near its end
Will it be very long
Well now the storm is finally over
And look here I still stand
As the sun shines down upon me
My Maker reveals to me His plan
He shows me that through the wind the rain and storm
How He was pruning me
Purging away the parts that are weak
And unable to fight against the enemy
He did it so I could endure
The test of another storm
So even though I may look tattered and torn
I still stand tall in the beauty of God's perfect form

Never Moving

Help me not to move Lord
Unless it's of Your will
Cause me to be quiet
And in Your peace be still
Let me never waver
From the place in which You've set me
For when I step out of Your will
I become blinded and cannot see
I see only what the world sees
A world filled with pain and darkness
Hearing only words of despair and sorrow
When I'm not living in Your righteousness
I need to see through Your eyes
And hear the stillness of Your voice
It's feeling the gently beat of Your heart
That causes me to make the right choice
Flowing in Your Spirit
Like the gentle breeze in the early morning hour
So cool and softly it blows
But yet filled with Your glory and power

Deeper Still

My soul cries out to You
Spirit of the living God
My soul cries out to You
Spirit of the living God

As deep calls unto deep
Take me deeper still
As deep calls unto deep
I want to know Your will

As deep calls unto deep
My soul cries out to You
As deep calls unto deep
Take me deeper still

Take me deeper Lord
Take me deeper
Deeper, deeper still
Take me deeper Lord
Take me deeper
My soul cries out to You

The Place of Transition

Lord I hear You calling me
From my state of selfishness
To a deeper place of transformation
And Your righteousness
The transition is so hard to make
Because of my desire to please my soul
It means I'll have to lay down some things
And give You full control
I need Your strength to do this
And a fresh anointing on my life
Pour Your oil of gladness over me
And burn up all the strife
Cause me to take my eyes off of me
And seek Your will and Your desire
As You can transform me into pure gold
Help me to endure the pressures
Of the refiners fire

In The Potter's Hands

Laying in the potter's hands
Is a formless lump of clay
Within my mind I wonder
Will He make something or throw it away
It's broken into pieces
And shattered from the fall
It seems so pointless to use it
Does it have any worth at all
Then I watch as His hands
So gentle and warm
Start to mold and shape it
Into somewhat of a form
So what's so special about that lump of clay
Doesn't He realize it's not even real
Then to my amazement He takes the time
To mold it on His potter's wheel
As He handles it ever so cautiously
That little piece of clay becomes whole
As He pours His heart into its lifeless state
It becomes a living soul
Now I begin to see that lifeless piece of clay
Is really you and me
It's in that state of nothingness
That He can mold us to what He wants us to be
So please don't take me off the potter's wheel
Until Your work is through
This is just the start of a process
To make me more like You

From The Wheel To The Fire

You've taken me off Your potter's wheel
And placed me in the fire
Where You say I'll be cleansed and purified
To become what You desire
So why am I here Lord
When I was so comfortable in Your hands
Where You were gently molding me
To fit into Your perfect plan
So now as I question why Lord
And You speak to me Your Word
While I'm still seeking answers
Your gentle voice is heard
The fire is to strengthen you
So if you should ever fall
You won't shatter into pieces
But on my name you'll call
It cleanses out all the impurities
Those that are not seen within
It burns up worldly desires
That would cause your heart to sin
The refiner's fire is a place of transition
To purify and make you strong
So when the transformation is complete
You'll be back in my arms where you belong

Possessing The Land

Where am I suppose to live
What land will I possess
Will it be a place
Of Your peace and righteousness
Does it really matter
Where this earthen vessel dwell
Just as long as it's in Your presence
And it's of Your will
It could be a mansion
Filled with riches beyond compare
But what does it really matter
If Your love isn't there
It could be a little shack
On a lonely dusty road
But if it's filled with Your glory
It won't look so old
Because it's not just the glitz and glamour
Of the outside that shows it's worth
But it's the Spirit on the inside
That counts here on this earth
The beauty on the inside
Will manifest in the outward appearance
So it can be a mansion or a shack that I possess
As long as You take up residence

The House Of The Righteous

I want to stand in the house of the righteous
The place where Your glory dwells
Abiding in the house of the faithful
As my testimony it tells
In Your presence living
Each and every day
Never stepping out of Your will
And in Your grace I'll stay
Surrounded by Your Spirit
As Your heart in me You confide
The place of refuge and assurance
That Your love for me will never be denied

It's In The Seed

A mighty rain can fall
From small gray cloud and skies
Out of a little egg
A majestic eagle flies
From a little acorn
Comes a might oak to give us shade
It's from a tiny seed
That all of this is made
I think it's so amazing
What a little seed can do
From just a few seeds
A harvest we reap
To see us long winters through
From a tiny baby
To the deliverer of our soul
He came to heal a seed of brokenness
And make our spirits whole
I think it's so amazing
What a tiny see can do
From just a tiny seed of love
Came salvation for me and you

A Moment of Eternity

Can I have just a moment Lord
A moment of Your time
I have something I want to give You
And I have something on my mind
Give me just a moment Lord
To sing to You my song of love
As You are seated in the heavenlies
So I set my affections on things above
I can't promise it won't take long
It's flooding the deepest parts of my soul
It will take all of eternity to tell You
Of my love for You for making me whole
My passion and desire to serve You
Burns so deep within my heart
So please Lord give me just a moment of eternity
Pouring my love on You is where I want to start

My Final Journey

When my journey on earth is over
And my life has its final end
Will others see my love for You was real
Or say it was just pretend
What will my life's impression be
Will I be counted as one of the faithful few
Did my life cause others to walk Your way
Or did they turn their back on You
Did I allow You to pour out of me
Your never-ending mercy and grace
So that it caused others
To want to seek Your face
Was my life a testimony
Until my final breath
Did others see I loved You
Even unto death
I pray my life has been a reflection
Of a God of power and love
In the beauty and holiness
Of our Heavenly Father above
So that our final journey
Together we will be
Walking hand in hand
With Him by the Crystal Sea

Words From My Most Secret Place are poems that were written when at times I felt like all hope was lost. They were times when the Lord had me in a desert place, which caused me to hunger and thirst after Him. I came to know the wilderness experience as a place of totally trusting in God. I soon came to realize that God had me in the wilderness for a specific reason. It was to call me away to a place of intimacy with Him. He wanted me to be alone with Him.

And He said unto them, Come ye yourselves apart into a desert place, and rest a while.
(Mark 6:31)

Did I Give It All

Well here I go again every emotion running wild
Flooding my soul with feelings like anger and despair
I thought I laid them down at the cross
But too many memories with the flesh I share
I thought I gave them all for You to do what You will
Then I could set my affections on things above
Did I really give them all to You
Or just the ones I thought You were worthy of
Did I give a few I thought You could handle
And yet I could still be in control
Then I wouldn't have to open up that secret place
That's buried deep within my soul
Did I give up all the hurt from the past
When I thought love would always last
What about the hate I feel
When I look in the mirror and don't like what I see
Believing I am fearfully and wonderfully made
Is it something that will ever come to be
Then there's the despair when I fall time after time
Never winning the fight
Depression comes because I never seem to gain ground
Walking around in vapors of silent tears day and night
What about the feelings of defeat that's a constant battle
As I walk around with a smile on my face
Wearing a mask of make believe
Feeling like a complete failure and a total disgrace
So Lord tell me where do I begin
How do I get rid of this disguise
Please Lord take me to that place
Where I see myself through Your eyes

Lay Down The Burdens

What's that Lord lay my burdens at the cross
I thought I did that time and time again
But it seems they keep coming back to torment me
When will it ever end
I've given You all I thought I had
Now all of a sudden they're back
What's missing Lord am I not hearing Your voice
Or is it trust I lack
I've given You a lot at least I thought I had
Did I pick them up and put them back in my secret place
It seems You keep giving them back to me
You said You would take them as I come and seek Your face
I know I've given them out of frustration and anger
When I said take them Lord was I not meaning what I say
Giving them out of frustration isn't working
So tell me is there another way
As I sit alone in silence
And listen to Your still small voice
I'm beginning to understand
Giving them out of anger is not the right choice
As I lay them at Your feet
I'll have to bow and surrender my will
Ridding myself of foolish pride
My selfish ambitions and flesh to kill
As I come and kneel at the cross
A place of obedience and trust
If I want freedom from all that hinders me
Kneeling at the cross isn't an option but a must
So here I am Lord once again with all I have
I'm tired of walking around with a broken heart
I bow down and surrender in obedience to Your will
So the healing process can start

Nothing To Give

I feel so empty inside
Nothing to give
How can I put out
When I don't see a reason to live
What's my reason and purpose
Where does my destiny lie
How can I help others
When silent tears I cry
What's the answer to mend this broken heart
Can it be healed from its hurt and pain
I want to cry out to any one who understands
But no one does so I refrain
Unless they have been there
They will never know the sting
They don't know what it feels like
To be asked to give when you don't have anything
So I just keep on going and pretending
That everything's all right
Somewhere in the darkness
There has to be a glimmer of light

What's Come Over Me

Well another day is here and no joy to be found
I can't even find a reason to smile
I'm so deep in sadness and despair
Digging myself out is going to take awhile
Went through the day defeated inside
Even put on a different face
So no one could see the hurt I hide
Besides all they will say is
"Let it go" or "Give it to God"
Why don't they try walking with me
This lonely path I trod
I don't think they could handle it
It's easier to give their opinion and advise
They might try walking with me once
But I know they would not do it twice
I know these words sound harsh
But I'm not trying to be
I don't even like these feelings
What's happening Lord what's come over me
There was a time not long ago
I felt so good about me and really loved life
But now that's all gone
It's just heaviness and strife
I know that You're there Lord
And I know that You care
So I'm not giving up
With You my heart I can share
I don't have to be afraid to show my true feelings
I know I can be real with You
Because I know You love me
And Your promises are amen and true
Please give me back that joy and passion
That burned within me like a raging fire
Let it flood my soul like a rushing river
So that serving You is my only desire

Dead Idols or A Living God

Tell me where does your passion lie
Is it in what the world has to give
Does your heart long for dead idols
And those things that will never live
Are your lustful eyes seeking
For what will give your soul pleasure
To where you are so burdened down
With dead idols and earthly treasure
You're walking down the wrong path
Because all it's riches can never bring you life
It's a path of death and destruction
Heartache and strife
There needs to be a change
You need to seek life from a living God
Lay down those dead idols
On a new path of life you must trod
Stir up the passion of Christ that lies within you
And let Him transform your heart and mind
Lay down those dead idols
New life in a living God you will find

Words From My Heart To Yours is a collection of poems that the Lord gave me for specific people in my life. Some I knew who they were for immediately while others God showed me in specific ways. God has put us in one another's lives for a reason. You are all such a vital part of my life. I pray these poems were an encouragement to you.

And if one prevail against him, two shall withstand him; and a threefold cord is not quickly broken.
(Ecclesiastes 4:12)

My Husband My Friend

We started out in life
Not really knowing each other
But as time went on
We learned the characters
Of one another
Our love and trust grew
Strong through out the years
It flourished with our laughter
And was watered by our tears
Because this love we had
Grew very deep and strong
God saw fit to bless us
And our daughter and son came along
Committed to God and our family
As we fulfilled God's plans
He kept us through the years
In His gentle loving hands
Although things in our lives have changed
This three-strand cord cannot sever
Because God's love and care for us
Is everlasting and forever
I know our love still stands strong
And will be until the end
Because I have someone special
My husband and my friend

Dedicated to my husband, Tony, a true friend.

God's Rose

When God made the rose
He had you in mind
For it's beauty and elegance
Are rare to find
Red is for your courage
As you fight against sin
White is for purity
Of your heart within
Yellow is for your strength
As you face each day
Pink is for God's peace
You have along life's way
When wind and rain come along
Against the storm you stand strong
Though the storm be rough
When it's all said and done
You're able to smile
And reflect God's son
All these characters exist in you I find
For when God made the rose
He had you in mind

Dedicated to my beautiful daughter Amanda, an awesome woman
of God.

God's Priceless One

There's something about your name
That I have come to see
It's not just in the name
But what you've come to be
Nathaniel means "God has given"
Anthony "A Priceless Treasure"
That is what you are to me
A gift from God that cannot be measured
He's placed within you something
That no one else can give
I draw from you its strength
And it causes me to live
It seems you grew up way to fast
And didn't have much of a childhood
You had some big shoes to fill
But the trying times you withstood
Now you've grown into a fine young man
Full of love and integrity
Born with a heart of compassion
And with all sincerity
So thank you son for pouring out
Gods love in all you do
I am so very proud to say
I have a son like you

Dedicated to my handsome son, Nathan, an awesome man of God.

My Unseen Hero

Dad, It seems I didn't have much time
To really get to know you
The Lord beckoned you home
And your time on earth was through
Not really understanding why
The Lord took you away
I walked around with an emptiness
Each and every day
Our years together were but few
When death knocked on your door
Not passing on any earthly treasures
Because it seemed we were quite poor
As life went on all I felt
Was deaths sting of hurt and strife
I wasn't until just recently
God showed me an unseen hero in my life
Now I see the riches you left
Can't compare to earthly treasure
Because the things you passed on to me
Bring me hope beyond its measure
You instilled in me your knowledge
Your wisdom and inner strength
A passion to seek the heart of God
And your never-ending faith
I received from you integrity
That earthly things can't give
I drew from you a desire to love others
That has taught me how to live
So now as I look at all these riches
I have begun to see
You had an unseen hero in God's only Son
That you passed on to me
So yes dad you are my hero
But I hope that you don't mind

That I pass these treasures on to my children
So an unseen hero they will find

Dedicated in loving memory to my father who left to me a legacy.

Because You Prayed

I remember when as a little child
You'd send me to Sunday School
I learned to hide God's Word in my heart
And of the "Golden Rule"
And I did because you prayed
You taught me of the love of Jesus
And to trust Him with all my might
As we prayed "Now I lay me down to sleep"
As you tucked me in each night
I can because you prayed
Then as a teen I did rebel
And from the Lord did stray
But His loving hand of protection was on me
That led me back to Him today
It was because you prayed
When as a young woman
As I started out in life
You knew the things I'd encounter
Like sorrow pain and strife
But I made it through the hard times
God's peace and victory to show
Within my heart without a doubt
This one thing I know
It was because you prayed
Now I am a grown woman
And life can still be hard
But you taught me how to get on my knees
And trust in His Holy Word
I can because you prayed
So now I applaud you mother
And give you honor that is due
I thank God for your faithfulness
And strength that's brought me through
You may not have earthly riches

That you would like to share
But the treasure that's inside of you
To this world does not compare
You've been my inspiration
As I live from day to day
I'll always treasure the things of God
You passed along the way
Because I know you still pray

Dedicated to my mother, a praying woman.

A Faithful Father's Love

Sometimes things in life happen
We don't quite understand
But as I look back on the yesteryears
I can see it was all in God's plan
He gave a special piece of Himself
To help come take care of me
I know this in my heart
Because His character in you I see
You possess some qualities
Of my Heavenly Father above
Although there are many
The greatest of these is *LOVE*
I know it couldn't have been easy
To take on a family of this fashion
But your heart was full of love
And a Godly *COMPASSION*
You've bring to me *JOY* and laughter
And cry with me when I was sad
You even look for ways to make *PEACE*
When I get upset or mad
I can still see you crying
As you walked me down the isle on my wedding day
I felt so proud to have you there
As you gently kissed me and gave me away
It's those little acts of *KINDNESS*
And showing that you care
You're always willing to lend a hand
When no one else is there
You've been so *FAITHFUL* all these years
And stood strong through life's tests
Because of your *UNSELFISH* love
I have been so blessed
I know I don't always show it
But your love to me is a treasure

Nothing in this world compares
Because your love cannot be measured

Dedicated to my step-father, Norm, who loves unconditionally.

A Sister's Prayer

Thank You Lord for my sister
And her loving caring ways
Thank You for the love we share
As we live from day to day
We've been through a lot together
And memories we share
Like the time I took the scissors
And cut off "Patty Play Pal's" hair
Sliding down poles together
Until they fell apart
Even when I blamed it on her
She forgave me from her heart
She accepts me for who I am
Nothing more and nothing less
She always encourages me
To give it my very best
She's been there through grief and sorrow
We've shared much laughter and many tears
She's been a sister of compassion
To help me overcome my fears
Through life's joys and pains
Never her love forsaking
She's been there with a hug
When my heart was aching
She's been an inspiration
In every kind of emotion
So thank You Lord for Your gift of love
My sister my friend
A love of endless devotion

Dedicated to my sister, Ellen, for believing in me.

God Will Find Your Praise

When it feels like there's darkness all around you
And no one sees or feels your pain
Just lift your voice toward heaven
And offer a sacrifice of praise

God will find your praise
God will find your praise
Just lift your voice toward heaven
And God will find your praise

He'll heal your hurt and lighten up the darkest way
He's reaching out to take away the pain
Just raise your hands toward heaven
And offer a sacrifice of praise

God will find your praise
God will find your praise
Just raise your hands toward heaven
For God will find your praise

He sees and feels the anguish you face from day to day
He'll lighten up the burdens along life's way
Just turn your head toward heaven
And offer a sacrifice of praise

God will find your praise
God will find your praise
Just turn your head toward heaven
For God will find your praise

Dedicated to my friend Linda C., remember He inhabits the praises
of His people.

Your House Your Home

Lord this is Your house
Please make it Your home
To live in and abide in
A holy place to come
Make this a temple
Filled with worship and praise
May it be open to You
All of my days
Let it be a place
For Your glory to rest
Filled with Your Spirit
For You to be blessed
Grant me the strength
To keep it clean and pure
May You find with in it
To be an open door
So as You dwell in this house
Please make it Your home
Fill it with love joy and peace
A holy place to come

Dedicated to Nancy C., whose tender heart toward God has
inspired this poem.

A Mother's Heart

Only God knows the love
Of a mother's heart
As you plead to Him from Your presence
Please don't let my son depart
In return He says
Don't you fret or fear a thing
For I have your son here
Safe beneath My wing
He knows the hardest thing
For a mother to do
Is to say Father, he's Yours
I give him to You
It's difficult to let go
And give God full control
But it's part of God's plan
For the salvation of his soul
As you go each day and see
Within him the war that rages
Anchor your trust
In the Rock of Ages
As a sparrow may fall
From its nest to the ground
God will gently pick him up
And His love will abound
Trust that the Lord is working
Everything for his good
And when the battle is over
You'll see the test of time he withstood
Even though it hurts to see him
Go through such heartache and strife
Nothing can blot out his name
Written in the Lamb's Book of Life
With God's strength and protection
He'll endure this trial and test

As you pray just remember
Under God's wing is also a place of rest

Dedicated to Christa B. who is a spiritual mom in every area of my life.

Reflections Of You

As I reflect upon my youth
And the childhood I once knew
I just can't help but remember
A very special love from you
Playing "Jacks" and cards and games
You even sat upon the floor
While I ate my "Cheez-It's"
From the "Five & Ten" cent store
The countless trips to the beach
To build castles in the sand
You being in my life
Was all part of God's divine plan
I even remember how
When I was afraid of storms
I'd run to you for comfort
And fall asleep within your arms
So with this poem I hope you see
Just what you really mean to me
For you are still as special today
As you were from the very start
I will always cherish
The love you placed within my heart

To my beautiful Aunt Ida. You are a very special part of my life.

At Jesus Feet

Come and sit at Jesus feet
And as you offer Him your life
He'll take away those things
That often try to cause you strife
Pour out your heart
And release the doubts and fears
You'll soon find peace
As you wash His feet with your tears
Like a child with her Father
He'll caress you in His arms
To shelter and protect you
And keep you safe from harm
He's such a loving Father
And wants only for you His best
So come and sit at Jesus feet
And enter into His rest

Dedicated to Pastor Betty, a beautiful, powerful woman of God.

Hold Onto His Hand

Sometimes the Lord will lead you
Down paths you don't understand
Just put your trust in Him
And hold tight to the Master's hand
At times you may feel lost
Or even all alone
And you may feel frightened
Because of the unknown
But your Father will never leave you
On soft or shifting sand
You'll never be forsaken
In a barren or desert land
There are times when He'll allow you
To walk through valleys low
To bring you to His holy mountain
For peace and victory to know
Just hold tight to your Fathers hand
As you walk each stride
For even when you feel all alone
He's right there by your side

Dedicated to Tom J. who held on to God's hand through a very
tough storm.

His Peace In The Midst Of Battle

You've gone to fight for our freedom
And bring peace to a troubled land
But as you're standing in the midst of battle
Hold tight to the Master's hand
As you defend our country
And war wages all around
Listen for His still small voice
And His peace will be found
He's bigger than any battle
And stronger than the enemy
So just hold tight to the Master's hand
As He leads you to victory

Dedicated to the men and women in Iraq.

All For You

I have come to tell you
Just how much I love you son
I went to the cross for you
As if you were the only one
I was beaten bruised and battered
A crown of thorns placed upon my head
It was all due to my love for you
That my blood was shed
I freely laid it down
And gave my life for you
I did this all to show you son
That my love was true
I conquered hell death and the grave
To give you power over the enemy
I rose again to bring you new life
For you to gain the victory
It's all because I love you son
My Spirit to you I impart
I poured my love inside of you
For you to know my heart
I did it all for you my son
So your soul would not be lost
You are my child my precious child
And I'd do it again at any cost

Dedicated to Jerome C. Remember His love ALWAYS.

As You Grow

I've known you from a little child
You were not quite two
I've watched you grow from year to year
How the time has flew
Through times of tears and laughter
I watch you growing into a man
And I just want to tell you
How proud of you I am
Growing up isn't easy
But remember as you walk life's way
God has a purpose and a plan for you
That's why you are here today
Always look to Him in prayer
For only He truly knows your heart
As you seek His wisdom and His counsel
New mercies He'll impart
As you grow He'll lead and guide you
And reveal to you His plan
He'll bring you into your destiny
As you hold tight to your Heavenly Father's hand

Dedicated to Cody B. on his 13th birthday.

Heavens Open Door

I saw the doors of heaven open
For the Lord to beckon you home
There to sing with the angels
Dancing around His glorious throne
He said come home my child
And enter into your rest
I know with what I've given you
You have done your very best
You life had been established
And your destiny fulfilled
It was hard for you to leave
But it is what God willed
What a beautiful place to be
Dancing on the clouds of glory
Sitting on our Father's lap
As He tells you of creations story
You've received your ultimate healing
That you've been longing for
A body total and complete
And suffering no more
So as you walk with our Daddy
Beside the Crystal Sea
Please do me a favor and take a moment
To give Him a hug from me

Dedicated in loving memory of my spiritual mom Kathy K. I miss
you.

A Graduation Prayer

I just want you to know that I am so proud of you
I know it wasn't always easy but you endured and made it
  through
So this is my prayer for you on this your Graduation Day
And that you will live it daily in each and every way

I pray...
  That as you face a whole new world you do it with integrity
  And as you grow into a beautiful young lady you'll seek your
    destiny

I pray...
  You'll always put God first in each and every circumstance
  And that you'll always remember you're not in our lives just by
    chance

I pray...
  You'll ask God to daily show you His purpose and plan for you
  And that you'll fully trust Him to always see you through

I pray...
  You'll build relationships with those that want only for you the
    best
  And when things seem to hard to handle you will turn to God for
    rest

I pray...
  Your heart will always be open to hear Gods still small voice
  So when life becomes a struggle you'll ask Him to help you
    make the right choice

I pray...
  You will know the choices you make don't just affect you
  But those that God has placed in your life are affected by it too

I pray...
>You'll always know you have been a blessing to me from the
>   start
>And through the years a place for you has grown deep within my
>   heart

Dedicated to Cara-Anne W. for her graduation. I knew you could
do it.

Look For The Lighthouse

Do you feel like you're drowning in the sea of life and can't find your way home? Just look for the lighthouse in the distant hills. It's there to guide you to a place of safety.

Even though the light may seem dim at first, as you near its shore it will get brighter and any obstacle in your way will become clearer to see so you can get around it and move it out of your way.

Tune you ear to the sound of the waves crashing against the rock that holds the lighthouse to solid ground. You'll know you're getting closer to the shore and you'll find shelter from the storm.

Listen for the bellow that peels through the darkness to lead you to safety. It may sound faint at first but as you become still it will get louder and the sounds of the world that try to drown you will be quieted by its call for you to come home.

Call for the keeper of the lighthouse. He holds the name above all names. It's a name that causes every knee to bow and every demon in hell to tremble. Angels sing His praises around the throne of glory and you can too. Just call it out. It can be a silent whisper from the deepest and darkest places of your heart to a shout that comes from the depths of your soul. No matter where it comes from or whatever the circumstance, He is there to answer your call.

His name is *Jesus.*

Dedicated to Linda B. my big sister and a great friend.

Becoming A Man Of Valor

Through the years as I've watched you grow
Into a fine young man
I've seen the Lord gently working in you
His marvelous and glorious plan
You've touched the hearts of many
By the simple things you do
I have been so blessed because of this
So this is my prayer for you…

I pray…
You never lose that special gift
That often makes me smile
Those crazy little faces have helped me
Make it through many a trial

I pray…
You'll always guard your heart and mind
Against the world and all its schemes
And that you'll always seek Gods face
As you dare to fulfill your dreams

I pray…
You'll always have the courage
To stand up for what is right
And that your heart stays tender
As life's battle you may fight

I pray…
As you become a mighty man of valor
Strong and powerful in God's way
May God's wisdom knowledge peace and joy
Grow deeper in you as you follow Him each and every day

Dedicated to Austin B. on his 13th birthday.

Words of Warfare is a collection of poetry concerning fighting the enemy and not each other. We need to take up our swords together and take back what is rightfully ours. We are over comers and conquerors through the mighty blood of Jesus and the gates of hell cannot and will not prevail against it.

For the weapons of our warfare are not carnal, but mighty through God to the pulling down of strong holds; Casting down imaginations, and every high thing that exalteth itself against the knowledge of God, and bringing into captivity every thought to the obedience of Christ.
(2 Corinthians 10:4-5)

Vapors of My Past

I degree and declare my past is just a vapor. It has no control over me. I have spoken to the dry bones and have chosen life over death. I now have and claim the power and authority God has given me to use my past *as I will.*

I will to no longer use it as a means of manipulation to get what I want or to use it as a means to satisfy my soul, which is my mind, will and emotions.

From this day forward *I will to* no longer allow my past to interrupt my future. It will no longer disrupt the plan and purpose God has for my life. My past will not define who I am or who I will become. The only involvement I will allow the past to have in my life is to be a stepping-stone toward my advancement in the Kingdom of God. It will be used as an instrument to encourage others and as a testimony of the power and love of God in my life.

My past will no longer display sorrow or pain, anger or fear. It will not reflect bitterness or hatred. *I will for it to* be used as a testimony that will display mercy and grace, righteousness and joy, peace and forgiveness.

I am a new creation and old things have become new. I don't care if it was thirty or forty years ago or just yesterday. It is still the past. Yesterday's experiences are old. *I will to* not allow the negative things that happened even yesterday to have control over me or to have an affect on me today or disrupt what God's will is for me tomorrow.

I will to now see myself as a new creation each and every day. Today is a new day leading me into a future filled with faith, hope, love and prosperity.

From this day forward *I will to* no longer see it as my past but as God given life experiences and testimonies to help teach and train others. They will be used as tools to build up and establish the Kingdom of God in others lives.

I will to relinquish the soul ties that have been used to destroy and tear up the pathway that leads to my destiny. *I will to* reverse the curses that have been spoken into my life from my childhood to the present.

I will to cling to the ones that God has placed in my life for covenant relationship. They are the ones that will walk with me and love me with God's unconditional love. They will help me to make and keep my path straight. They are the ones that will not dig up the old man but will feed my spirit with life and hope. They will be the ones that will help lay the foundation that leads to my destiny and they will have a strategic part in fulfilling the purpose and plan God has for my life.

I declare that we will use our life experiences to help pave the way for our destinies as we walk together in covenant relationship. We will not keep our life experiences to ourselves but we will share them to establish other covenant relationships to further the Kingdom of God in their lives.

Many have been called to design God's divine purpose and plan for my life but only a few have been chosen by God to be woven into or graphed into the pattern so that my destiny and purpose in Him can be fulfilled.

Takin' It Back

You tied my feet in shackles
And bound them up with chains
Taken away my healing
And caused my body to ache with pain
You've stolen from me joy
And plagued my soul with sorrow
But Satan I've had enough
I'm takin' it back today
Not waiting for tomorrow

Cause today's my day of freedom
I've called upon God's name
Today's my day of deliverance
He taken away my shame

God has loosened up my shackles
And broken all the chains
He's given me back my healing
And taken away the pain
My soul's now filled with joy
No longer plagued with sorrow
Because I've had enough
I'm takin' it back today
Not waiting for tomorrow

Cause today's my day of freedom
I've called upon God's name
Today's my day of deliverance
He's taken away my shame

My Praise is a Weapon

I have a weapon for my warfare
It's a sacrifice of praise
I will lift my hands towards heaven
And my voice I'll raise
It pulls down the strongholds
That once had me bound
As I use my weapon
Deliverance is found

This weapon that I use
Is not a carnal thing
It cast down imaginations
And victory it brings
It is quick and mightier
Than a two edged sword
There is nothing more powerful
Than the Word of God

It goes before me in battle
To bring the victory
It divides and conquers
And destroys the work of the enemy
So as I fight the good fight
And stand upon His Word.
I'll use my praise as a weapon
And put my trust in the Lord

I'm An Over Comer

So what if you stumble
Or you slip and fall
You feel like you just can't cope
And your backs against the wall
There's some one right beside you
To lend a helping hand
He's there to pick you up
And lead you on when you just don't understand

Just don't give up and don't you dare give in
You're an over comer by the blood of the Lamb

When struggles come
And troubles weigh you down
You feel like you're in deep water
And you're going to drown
There's some one out there
To help pull you out
Reach for His hand
And get rid of that fear and doubt

Just don't give up and don't you dare give in
You're an over comer by the blood of the Lamb

Come on now say it with me

I'm an over comer
I have over come
His power is within me
I've over come by the blood of the Lamb

Armored Together

You need to turn your anger
On your real enemy
And stop directing it
At others and me
Because the things in your mind
Aren't really what they seem
It's just a trick of the enemy
And his lying scheme
Stop coming to me
With all your insecurities
And all your phony stuff
The devil's messing with your mind
Let's take a stand and say enough is enough
So if you're coming to me for help
I'll gladly take up my sword and fight
But if it's in a state of confusion and division
I'll come against those spirits with all my might
Be careful how you approach me
Because I can hear the battle cry
I have my weapons all in order
I'm not willing to sit back and watch you die
The enemy knows your worth
And to destroy your mind would give him pleasure
So if you're not willing to fight for it I am
Because I see in you a Godly treasure
So let's pick up our weapons together
And prepare to attack the rulers of darkness
Let's put on the whole armor of God
And stand for His truth and righteousness

Not Just a Wall

In each and every one of us
Are walls within our hearts
Some built high with strong foundations
And some are just at their start
Brick by brick we build them
Naming each and every one
Sometimes feeling proud of its creation
When it is finally done
Building up walls and calling them
By names other than what they really are
Calling it a wall of protection
So the offenses of life don't leave a scar
Can't you see that what you're building
Isn't really protecting you at all
But it's causing you to close yourself in
And making others to fall
While you're on one side
Feeling safe and secure
Others stumble in your darkness
Making their pathway unsure
So let's tear down that wall you call protection
Because it's only causing you strife
Use the broken pieces to build an altar
As a testimony of your life

All Glory And Honor Be To My Savior And Lord…

As From His Inner Chamber Comes Newness Of Life As He Speak To Me His Word.

I have seen You in the Sanctuary and beheld Your power and Your glory. Because Your love is better than life, my lips will glorify You. I will praise You as long as I live, and in Your name I will lift my hands.
(Psalms 63:2-4)

CPSIA information can be obtained at www.ICGtesting.com
Printed in the USA
BVOW040827070512

289468BV00001B/129/A